Being

What You've

BECOME

Being
What You've BECOME

THE MAKING OF A CHRISTIAN

STEPHEN MANLEY

Cross Style Press

BEING WHAT YOU'VE BECOME
© 2018 by Stephen Manley

First Published 1973
Revised Edition 2005
Third Edition 2009
Fourth Edition 2018

Published by Cross Style Press
Lebanon, Tennessee
CrossStyle.org

Edited by Delphine Manley

ISBN-10: 0-9987265-3-2
ISBN-13: 978-0-9987265-3-3

Printed in the United States of America.

CrossStyle.org

CONTENTS

PREFACE

Conserving the fruits of evangelism is a great concern of every dedicated Christian. The great need of the Christian is to "be" what he has "become" — a true follower of Christ. "Becoming" a Christian is what happens at the altar of prayer or the place of repentance, but "being" a Christian is what takes place on the street of living

The intent of this book is to encourage and strengthen you in "being what you've become." May God help us all to this end.

— Stephen Manley

I

BE A CHRISTIAN

As one views the scope of belief as found in the evangelical church, one sees two major concepts of thinking. One concept is the "giving" experience of Christianity; the other is the "being" experience. These two concepts are in distinct contrast to each other.

Most of us who call ourselves Christians have been a part of the "giving" experience concept. We have had it drilled into our minds until it shows up in our prayers, our testimonies, our witnessing, and our defeat. Defeat is listed last because that is where most of us spend our time. If not in defeat, at least in struggling with such heavy problems that we have nothing left over for constructive action. I believe this "giving experience" to be a false concept!

The basic concept is that one comes to a Christ who has all of the supplies for us. He stands behind a counter called an altar, and behind Him is shelf after shelf of spiritual "goodies" which all of us need. We come to this place of supply and place our order for what we need at that moment. If we are in need of strength, we say "Jesus, GIVE me strength." If we need forgiveness, we say "Jesus, GIVE me forgiveness." What happens then is that a pound or yard is measured out of the item needed most. One takes it from there to use it on the street, only to discover that the item was not what he needed at all, for he meets an unknown circumstance. Or perhaps one uses what he received, only to discover that at the crucial moment he runs out and ends in defeat. One must run back to the supply house called the church and get renewed stock. This is the "giving" experience.

The "being experience" is vitally different. It shouts the truth that Jesus does not want to give you anything; rather He wants to BE something within you. Jesus does not want to GIVE you forgiveness; He wants to BE Forgiveness within you. Jesus does not want to GIVE you strength; He wants to BE Strength within you.

I fear we have been wrapped up in what Jesus can do for us, rather than who Jesus is. Jesus said (John 14:6), "I am the way." He is not going to be a road map or a road sign to point us in the right direction. He is the Road Himself. Jesus went on to say, "I am the life." 1 John 5:12 says, "He that hath the Son hath life; and he that hath not the Son of God hath not life." Life is a by-product of the presence of Jesus "being" within you. Jesus said, "I am the truth." He does not want to write the truth down for you. He is the Truth and He wants to BE Truth within you.

This basically means one thing — the need of your life is singular. You do not need happiness, joy, peace, forgiveness, life, truth, strength, etc. You need Jesus. When one possesses Him, all of these things are possessed as a by-product of His great presence! Therefore, the Christian experience is the presence of another Person — God — inside your life. He must dwell in the inward functionings of your life. A Christian is not one who "does," but one who "has"; therefore, he IS because Jesus IS.

It is significant to note that the writings of the Apostle Paul are filled with the "being" concept. A great scripture which will introduce this to us is found in the book of Colossians. The hinge or focal point to which everything in this book fixes itself is in chapter 1, verse 27. It is here that Paul states "Christ in you" as his theme. What a theme it is! The result of the indwelling of a personal Christ inside your body is that He shares in every 24-hour experience.

Everything before this focal point of verse 27 tells us who Jesus is. It is a description of the tremendous Christ who has come to live within. Everything after verse 27, especially in chapter 2, tells us the results of containing Him within our lives. In Colossians 1:13, Paul introduces his subject by using the phrase "his dear Son" at the end of the verse. Beginning at verse 14, he describes "his dear Son".

REDEEMER
(Colossians 1:14)

"…in whom we have redemption through His blood, the forgiveness of sins."

Here is the entire redemption program wrapped up in one Person. It has not been spread out in the acts of many, but has been centralized into the great Christ. In the Book of Revelation (5:11-12), there are the voices of "ten thousand times ten thousand and thousands of thousands; saying… 'Worthy is the Lamb that was slain…'" Before the scene closes, every being in the heavenlies and all upon earth are wrapped up in Jesus, the Redeemer. Who has come to be Redemption within you 24 hours a day? It is the Christ.

VISIBLE IMAGE
(Colossians 1:15)

*"He is the image of the invisible God,
the firstborn over all creation."*

God the Father has not been seen. John 1:18 tells us "No man hath seen God at any time; the only begotten Son, which is in the bosom of the Father, he hath declared Him." The invisible God has become visible. He has identified with us. Men slapped Him on the back; they felt His flesh. Jesus is God and He has been known. Who has come to be God within you 24 hours every day? It is Jesus!

FIRSTBORN
(Colossians 1:15, 18)

"He is the image of the invisible God, the firstborn over all creation....And He is the head of the body, the church, who is the beginning, the firstborn from the dead, that in all things He may have the preeminence."

Verse 15 tells how He is "the firstborn of every creature" (KJV). I do not understand this except that there is something so great going on in the person of Christ that it affects every living creature on every level. Then Paul narrows it down to say in verse 18 that He is "the firstborn from the dead." When He identified with man, it was to be an eternal identification. He became the very first man to have the new, resurrected body that all Kingdom men are going to have. He has already paved the way. Who is the One who has come to indwell? It is Jesus, who has gone before and knows the way. I need not fear, for He is my indwelling Companion.

CREATOR
(Colossians 1:16)

"For by Him all things were created that are in heaven and that are on earth, visible and invisible, whether thrones or dominions or principalities or powers. All things were created through Him and for Him."

He created it all — "visible and invisible." Nothing is but what has His touch on it, for it came through Him. Even your life is a result to His power. His creation is but a small, inadequate measuring rod of His greatness. Think of the fact that it is this God of tremendous power Who has come to be contained within your life! The gigantic, immense God of all creation has come to indwell and to share your life every day! Walk in confidence.

CONSISTOR
(Colossians 1:17)

"And He is before all things, and in Him all things consist."

Someone keeps things from flying apart. The atoms which make up everything around you are in constant motion. When an atom flies apart to bump other atoms and causes a chain reaction, we have the devastation of the atom bomb. Who stands with His hand on a universe keeping things together? None other than the very One who has come to live inside you. Certainly this Jesus can hold you together in any circumstance.

HEAD
(Colossians 1:18)

"And He is the head of the body, the church, who is the beginning, the firstborn from the dead, that in all things He may have the preeminence."

This word means "chief." Jesus is the Chief of His Church. Paul expressed his concept of the Church in terms of a body. No doubt this is what he is referring to in this verse. Christ is the Head of the living organism of the united believers. Each believer fits into the proper place as put there by the Head. Each one has a part to play in the functioning of this organism. This is important as it relates to the structured organizations. While you are not under the dictates of man, you are under the control of the Head, who wants to use you in your local organization. This Head is guiding you from within.

PREEMINENT
(Colossians 1:18)

"And He is the head of the body, the church, who is the beginning, the firstborn from the dead, that in all things He may have the preeminence."

What can one say except this Christ is Number One? He has top priority! He is the Causer of all that has been caused, who has never been "caused" Himself. He is the

One beyond whom you cannot go. When He comes to indwell your life, He comes as the preeminent One. He demands first place in your life. This is the Jesus within.

FULLNESS
(Colossians 1:19)

"For it pleased the Father that in Him all the fullness should dwell…"

This verse relates to chapter 2, verse 9. Here is the declaration that jam-packed into the person of Christ is the entirety of God, and that this Christ is jam-packed into you. The Christ you contain is not some low man on the totem pole. His is Top Brass!

PEACEMAKER
(Colossians 1:20)

"…and by Him to reconcile all things to Himself, by Him, whether things on earth or things in heaven, having made peace through the blood of His cross."

The conflicts are arrested due to His coming. As surely as His spoken voice calmed the raging sea, so His presence stills the inward tension in pressured surroundings. The Peacemaker has come to indwell you.

RECONCILER
(Colossians 1:20-21)

"…and by Him to reconcile all things to Himself, by

*Him, whether things on earth or things in heaven,
having made peace through the blood of His cross.
And you, who once were alienated and enemies
in your mind by wicked works, yet now He has
reconciled..."*

The word "reconcile" means "to bring back together". It is the picture of God and man being separated due to the great chasm of sin. That chasm has been bridged by Christ and we are reconciled. We, who had no chance of even sneaking into the presence of God, now walk boldly in to meet Him face-to-face! We do so because of the Reconciler who has come to indwell us.

How significant would it be to be indwelt by Jesus Christ if He lacked power, authority, and supremacy? Paul's description of the Christ which we just studied shows Christ to be tremendous. He is fantastic, beyond what we have ever dreamed. We have the staggering, unbelievable opportunity of not just talking about Him, but actually containing Him within our very bodies!

One thing is for certain: If a Christ such as described comes within to live on a 24-hour basis, it will make a difference. There *must* be results. These results are what Paul tells us about as he continues to write after verse 27.

WISDOM
(Colossians 2:3)

*"...in whom are hidden all the treasures
of wisdom and knowledge."*

All the truth and knowledge of the universe is wrapped up in Christ. If there is any truth any place, it is due to His revelation. Man existed totally in fear and superstition until there came revelation from above. This revelation climaxed in the person of Christ. Now you have this Christ within you Who gives you total access to this wisdom. The very wisdom of God saturating your mind to give direction to every movement!

PATHWAY
(Colossians 2:6)

"As you therefore have received Christ Jesus the Lord, so walk in Him…"

He is our pathway. You need not worry about the curve which may present itself in the future, for He is that Curve. Paul shares with us in Romans that all things work together for good to them that love God and are called according to His purpose. You can abide in perfect faith, aware that God is handling every situation to the maximum good for your life. The future is secure in Him.

STRENGTH
(Colossians 2:7)

"…rooted and built up in Him and established in the faith, as you have been taught, abounding in it with thanksgiving."

We have the strength that we need for each day because God, who is Strength, *is* indwelling us. As you have turned your life over to Him, He has turned the strength of His person over to you. If your strength is not yours, but His within you, then you are as strong as God is strong. Tell me what can defeat God and I will tell you what can defeat you!

The temptation that brings God down is the only one that can bring you down, if His strength has become yours as He is within you.

COMPLETION
(Colossians 2:9-10)

"For in Him dwells all the fullness of the Godhead bodily; and you are complete in Him, who is the head of all principality and power."

Paul injects a summary at this point. It is as if he is afraid of leaving something out of this list. So he wraps them all up in one great statement about our completeness in Christ. Many are looking for just one more thing, or experience, or achievement. Total surrender to the person of Christ, which allows His full presence to be within, is the climactic completion. There is no need beyond His fullness. You need not look further; the need of your life, then, is simply for Christ within.

CIRCUMCISION
(Colossians 2:11)

"In Him you were also circumcised with the circumcision made without hands, by putting off the body of the sins of the flesh, by the circumcision of Christ..."

As a by-product of this indwelling Christ comes His

purity. It is not achieved; it is shared. One does not strive to have it; one must surrender to have it given. It is not quantity of outward acts; rather it is quality of the indwelling Christ sharing His nature with you. When Moses saw the bush that was burning and heard the voice telling him that the ground was holy, he no doubt wondered what made that mountain dirt holy. Yesterday it had not been holy, but today it was. What made the difference? It was the presence of God. Holiness is derived from His presence. Purity of life comes because of the Spirit of this tremendous Christ within our lives.

DEATH — RESURRECTION
(Colossians 2:12)

"…buried with Him in baptism, in which you also were raised with Him through faith in the working of God, who raised Him from the dead."

The death-resurrection process is in all of the writings of the Apostle Paul. He tells us that through total surrender we die with Jesus. His death was our death, and in Christ we experience the death which is the penalty for our sins. If by faith we die with Him, then we are alive in Him. It is co-crucifixion and co-resurrection. This resurrection happens now. It is the new resurrected life of Jesus within you sharing Himself. You are alive because He is alive within you. Life is not something you have to pump up; it is the by-product of the fullness of Christ.

QUICKENING
(Colossians 2:13)

"And you, being dead in your trespasses and the uncircumcision of your flesh, He has quickened [made alive] together with Him, having forgiven you all trespasses…"

I used to think that quickening was something like sitting on a tack. When one comes up yelling, one could say, "I have been quickened." I found that this is the kind of experience we often have in our spiritual lives. We get these jabs every now and then which give us a big spurt, but they last only for a while. This is a far cry from what Paul is speaking about. Paul actually states "quickened together with Him." This is the indwelling of Christ saturating your life, giving a constant and consistent state of aliveness.

FREEDOM
(Colossians 2:16)

"So let no one judge you in food or in drink, or regarding a festival or a new moon or sabbaths…"

The indwelling Christ brings a relaxed living experience. Many are "uptight" about do's and don'ts. Paul is not teaching a long list of things to do to be pure, but rather he stresses surrender, which is BEING pure through Christ. Those who are "uptight" about legalism end up not possessing the purity in attitude and inward life. Paul says that we are not to get squeezed into this trap. Let us be Christ-like because of the Christ who is shining through our lives and who is controlling our actions.

REALITY
(Colossians 2:17)

"…which are a shadow of things to come, but the substance is of Christ."

The life of the Old Testament legalist was simply a shadow from the real object. We knew the shadow but now we know the real object. One will not be content with silhouettes when the real objects are available. The real object is Christ in His indwelling presence. It is the real thing! Come to reality!

BODY
(Colossians 2:19)

"…and not holding fast to the Head, from whom all the body, nourished and knit together by joints and ligaments, grows with the increase that is from God."

The body is a functioning unit. It is one thing to be a segregated Christian off in the shadows; it is another thing to be integrated and plugged into a living organism of hundreds and thousands of people who have this same indwelling Christ. We are one in the Spirit; we are one in the Lord.

This has to be the most fantastic experience of a lifetime! Meditate on these things. See who He is and what you can be; then bow at His feet in total surrender.

BOOK OF COLOSSIANS

Central Message:
"Christ in You" (Colossians 1:27)

WHO HE IS
(1:13-26)
1. Redeemer (v. 14)
2. Visible image (v. 15)
3. Firstborn (v. 18)
4. Creator (v. 16)
5. Consistor (v. 17)
6. Head (v. 18)
7. Preeminent (v. 18)
8. Fullness (v. 19)
9. Peacemaker (v. 20)
10. Reconciler (vv. 20-21)

RESULTS OF HIS INDWELLING
(2: 1-19)
1. Wisdom (v.3 - mind)
2. Pathway (v. 6 - future)
3. Strength (v. 7 - daily living)
4. Completion (v. 9-10)
5. Circumcision (v. 11 - purity)
6. Death-Resurrection (v. 12 - life)
7. Quickening (v. 13)
8. Freedom (v. 16)
9. Reality (v. 17)
10. Body (v. 19)

II

BE ALIVE

Probably the most important word in the Gospel of John is the word "life." Love is important to John, but life takes precedence over it — for without life there can be no love. John stresses belief, but only because it is a means to the end, which is life (John 20:31). In the 12 verses which are the consideration for this study (John 6:47-58), the word "life" is used 11 times. One gets the idea that John is trying to tell us something!

SUMMARY
(John 6:47)

"Most assuredly, I say to you, he who believes in Me has everlasting life."

Jesus is speaking in these verses. This part of His message is really the conclusion. What has been happening is that Jesus has been delivering quite a message to a large crowd. There was a group of fellows who sat on the back seat and talked during the message instead of really giving their minds to comprehension. So, in verse 43, Jesus had to tell them to keep still because they were getting confused about the things He was trying to tell them. Jesus then proceeds to tell them exactly what He has already told them, only in shorter form.

He begins verse 47 with a summary of everything He has told them and is going to tell them. His first two words are: "Verily, verily." These literally mean, "Shut up and listen; this is important." He proceeds to give a one-sentence sermon; "He that believeth on Me hath everlasting life."

Many are talking about eternal life after death or when Jesus comes again, but what of eternal life now? I certainly do not want to wait until then to receive eternal life. A proper biblical concept is the reality of eternal life running within our beings in present tense terms. Jesus used the word "hath." That means now! Eternal life is much more than just the absence of death! It is much beyond the state of existence. It carries with it the whole impact of meaning to life: purpose for living, happiness through destiny, and discovery of the "why." Note that Jesus says all of these hang upon the fact of believing. I fear we know little about this kind of belief in this day. It is not the shallow acknowledgment of certain facts; rather it is convinced belief that carries through into total surrender. One does not believe unless one surrenders. Nothing will suffice in Christianity but total surrender to Christ.

I AM
(John 6:48)

"I am the bread of life."

After the summary, Jesus begins to build a structure which leads to life. It is exciting to note the foundation point of the structure. "I am the bread of life." Christ is the Beginning Point. Not what He can do for you or what He can give to you, but what He can BE within you! This is the solid foundation upon which everything worthwhile rests. Christianity rises or falls upon the character of its God.

Moses was confronted by God at a burning bush to go to Pharaoh and demand freedom for God's people. Now who was Pharaoh? He was just the number one man in the whole known civilization. Some people considered him their god, and he was inclined to agree with them. Moses said to God, "If I go down there, Pharaoh is going to ask me where I get the authority to tell him what to do, since there is no authority greater than his. I shall tell him God sent me; but then he will ask me concerning Your name. What is Your name, God?" God's reply to Moses' question was, "I am that I am." In the Hebrew, it is a verb of being. No one has a verb for a name. No one is called "Mr. Is" or Mr. Are." No one, that is, except God. For the essence of His being is life. What He is is existence. The texture of His being is life. The intricate pattern of His soul's makeup is living. This is the Christ who confronts our lives. This One turned to a crowd and said: "I am the bread of life." He is the Essence of living that He might BE living in you.

PROMISE
(John 6:49)

*"Your fathers ate the manna in the wilderness,
and are dead."*

Jesus continues by illustrating His message. He gives an example from the Old Testament that His crowd would understand. The manna (Exodus 16:15) that God rained down from heaven was a symbol of life. It was a type of that Living Bread that was to come. It was a promise by God of Bread that would be given that would not have to be gathered daily, but that, once eaten, would produce continuous living.

PROMISE FULFILLED
(John 6:51)

"I am the living bread which came down from heaven. If anyone eats of this bread, he will live forever; and the bread that I shall give is My flesh, which I shall give for the life of the world."

Jesus no doubt was shouting when He came to this point in His message! For the promise had been given in the Old Testament; but now before their very eyes, that promise had been fulfilled. "Wait no longer; I am here," was His message. Jesus had been rained down from heaven in the early hours of redemption.

PREPARATION
(John 6:51)

"I am the living bread which came down from heaven. If anyone eats of this bread, he will live forever; and the bread that I shall give is My flesh, which I shall give for the life of the world."

But wait; even manna needs to be prepared. I personally am a butter-and-jam man. I have been known to interrupt a fancy banquet to ask for a jar of jam. Bread must be properly prepared with adequate butter and jam before it is eaten. Even Jesus Himself could not be proper Food for our lives until there had been adequate preparation. His preparation was the butter of the Cross and the jam of the Resurrection.

FOOD
(John 6:55, 48)

"For My flesh is food indeed, and My blood is drink indeed.... I am the bread of life."

When the preparation is completed, then proper food with proper taste is presented. The banquet table is spread and the Food is Christ! He is filled with the proper vitamins and minerals; He is the Nourishment which is adequate for life.

EATING
(John 6:56)

*"He who eats My flesh and drinks My blood
abides in Me, and I in him."*

Now comes the participation from you; up until this time you have been a spectator. Now you must partake of Him. This is the act of the exposure of your entire system to Him. When you partake of physical food, it is digested and its nourishment is sent to every part of the system. This must be true of the Bread of Life. You cannot partake of Him and expect Him to affect the religious life without entering into the entire social life. You dare not try to keep Him boxed up in your prayer language and think He will not affect the jokes you tell. The total life is under His influence. This is why it takes total surrender to the Bread of Life.

INDWELLING
(John 6:56)

*"He who eats My flesh and drinks My blood
abides in Me, and I in him."*

Jesus explains that this eating does not mean partaking of Communion. Rather it is the indwelling of the person of Christ within your body, participating in your total life. This brings us back to our basic teaching: Christianity is a "Be In." It is Jesus Christ being within you what He is...He is Life. Therefore, derived from His presence comes life for you.

How does this work in practical, every day life? If

Christ is Life, then life for you is hinged upon constant, continuous fellowship with Him. Martin Luther said, "The minute I consider the Christ and myself as two, I am lost." We must not be two; we must be one. Life is the by-product of this union.

To better illustrate, I must share my own experience. I was a sophomore in high school with tremendous doubts and uncertainty about my Christian experience. I really wanted to be a Christian, and had gone to an altar of prayer many times. But my experience was one of ups and downs with a nagging sense that things were not right.

One day I left the school and went to the church instead of eating my dinner. This was not a result of a religious service or revival meeting. It was not under the emotion of a quartet singing. I was simply a young man who was determined to find reality. With little emotion, but with determination, I got down on my knees to pray. Prayer was short and to the point. "Lord, I'm pulling the pin on You. This is it. Once and for all I am going to quit playing games with You. At this moment I surrender my *entire* self to be Your territory."

You see, the feeling area of my life had been one of my problems. I had been guided by what I felt, rather than by my commitment. Consequently my life was up and down instead of consistent in its output. Now that was settled. When I got up from that prayer, I didn't feel any different than when I came in. But, that did not matter now, for it was total surrender to Christ, regardless!

God shared with me a secret that day that has made the difference between night and day in my life. It is called "practicing His presence." I went back to the high school to begin a new way of living. Every time the bell rang at school, I would mentally stop and make myself be aware that I belonged totally to Christ and that He actually lived within me. Prayer is mental communion with God. If Christ has come to indwell my life that includes my mind. That means He is involved in *every* thought. One must be careful what one thinks, because we must literally do what Paul said: "Pray without ceasing."

The bell would ring at school and inside I would mentally say, "Hi, God. I'm glad You are in there. Stick with me; I need You." To be sure, sometimes I would forget to fellowship with Him when the bell rang. But I desperately worked at it, that I might become so used to doing it, that practicing His presence would become a habit for my life.

Another area that was important in this was the daily problems. I began to bring every daily problem to Christ, who was eagerly interested. This experience is God totally involved, which must include my problems. If He is not interested in my small problems, how can He be interested in my large ones?!

It worked something like this — "Hey, God, we've got a flat tire." Suddenly I was not having flat tires by myself, for Christ had become totally involved. "Hey, Lord, this is a hard test. Help me to remember." Suddenly it was Jesus who was helping me be at my best for His glory. Christ became involved in every problem: the jokes, the ball game, relationships with friends, and the dates. It was Jesus Christ saturating my life 24 hours a day! He became totally involved! It began when I totally surrendered, but it continued when I determined to live daily a surrendered life in His presence. I was to allow Jesus to BE what He wanted to be within me.

One day it dawned on me...I am really alive! Purpose, happiness, meaning, joy, good times have all come to my life. Where did they come from? They came from the indwelling presence of the Christ who had come to BE LIFE within me!

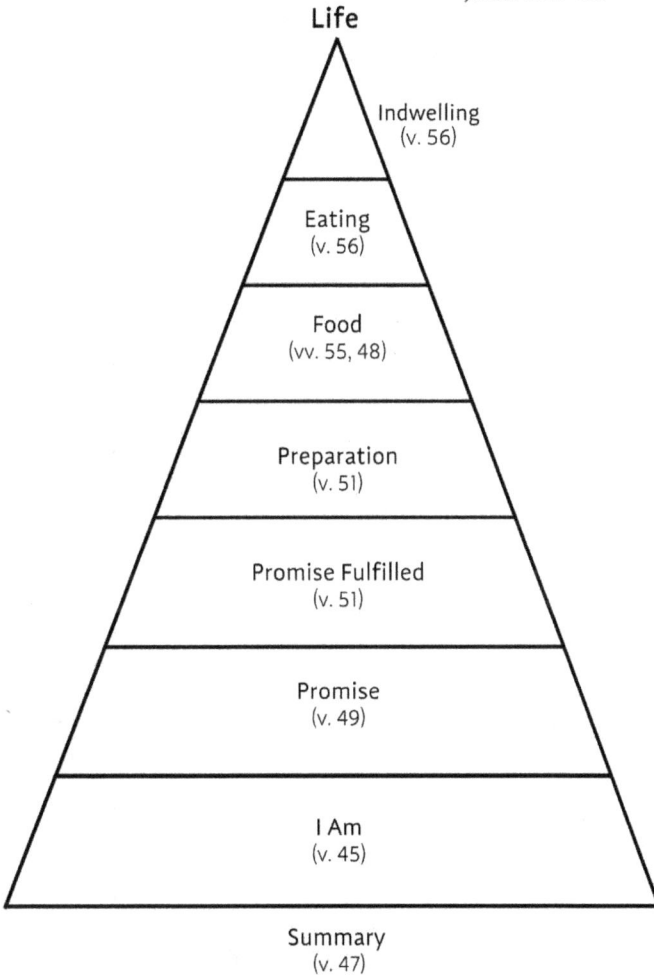

Be Alive

John 6:47-58

Life

Indwelling
(v. 56)

Eating
(v. 56)

Food
(vv. 55, 48)

Preparation
(v. 51)

Promise Fulfilled
(v. 51)

Promise
(v. 49)

I Am
(v. 45)

Summary
(v. 47)

III

BE PURE

"Is it right?" "What's wrong with dancing, shows, cards, premarital sex?" "The church *Manual* rules these out, but is that the final word?" "Isn't it just a matter of old-time traditions?" "What is the real standard for my life?" these are questions that are constantly bombarding youth workers everywhere. Argument upon argument goes out. Everyone gives his viewpoint, but no one seems convinced, just more confused.

It seems that there is a standard called holiness as presented in the Word of God that settles every question that is brought up against it. It answers so forcibly that one must see it for himself, until it is not a matter of opinion. What is this standard of holiness? It is actually found in Matthew 5:48. Here Jesus states that we must "BE perfect."

Now the word "perfect" is usually a relative word that we can rationalize around, but Jesus does not allow us to cop out here. He says that the perfection is to be like that of the Father in heaven! The standard is Godlikeness. Of course, as we rationalize, we know we shall be like Him when we get to heaven. But that is a cop-out, for Jesus says, "BE." This is a present-tense state of existence.

Notice that this perfection is a "being" state. Holiness is not achieved in terms of quantity of outward activities; rather it is a quality of inward life which is a "being" state.

If one has properly come to the state of "being", one must start at the beginning. Jesus starts us at verse 17 with the word "fulfilled." He relates to us that the law (standard) of God has not been done away with. It is not a process of tearing down or getting around, as has been our natural process. Rather it is fulfilled in the person of Christ. This means that Jesus has taken the entire Old Testament law and wrapped it up into a package called "Himself." *He* is the Standard. The law now is the person of Christ. If you want to know how to live, you must live like Jesus lives. His total life must be your total life. His manner of living must be yours. The Standard is Jesus.

When Jesus consumed this law into Himself, He did two things to it. Number one, He intensified this law. Jesus made the law worse; that is, it is more binding than it ever was in the Old Testament. What the Old Testament man could get by with, you cannot, due to this intensification of the law through the indwelling person of Christ in your life. Also, Jesus did a second thing to the law: He internalized it. That is, Jesus drove the law (standard) to our inward parts. In the Old Testament, the emphasis of the law was outward obedience; now it is inward motive. The Old Testament law emphasized the external action. Now the fulfilled law concerns itself with the internal purity, which is the controller of the external. Jeremiah prophesied that this very thing would happen. He said (Jeremiah 31:31-34) that a new day was coming in which God would put His law in the inward parts of His people and would write it upon their hearts. This would be the result of law fulfilled in the person of Christ and His indwelling through His Spirit.

Of course, for most of us, we would simply throw up our hands and say that it cannot be. We would rationalize, "If the standard is being like Jesus, then no one can arrive. Christianity has set up a standard that simply imposes a constant guilt complex due to a constant failure." But Jesus knew exactly what He was doing. He knew that we could not make it, so He told us of His indwelling Spirit, Who would *be* perfection within us. One begins to realize that Jesus is not only the Standard of the law, but He is the Keeper of that standard within us. What He wants us to do is to totally surrender ourselves to Him and allow Him to keep His law through us.

Note that Jesus did not instruct us to do perfect things (Matthew 5:48). Rather His instruction was to "be perfect." There is a vast difference between the two. To do is simply a legalistic conformity to a set pattern; but to be is an inward compulsion of motivation which produces a real individual. To do demands only rote action, but to be is the challenge of proper attitudes behind the action. To do is simply the absence of a wrong deed; but to be is the aggressive action of a burning heart. To do is nothing but duty; but to be is love shared. This is the call of a cross to our lives. We must not settle for the absence of wrong; rather, we must actually *be what we have become*!

Moses in his experience with a burning bush learned a valuable lesson. As he approached the bush, a voice spoke out to him, instructing him to remove his shoes due to the holiness of the ground. No doubt Moses wondered at such a statement. Yesterday he had been over this same ground, and a thousand times before that, but it had not been holy then. It was not special ground. Filled with rotting grass and leaves, it was just good old mountain ground. But suddenly it was holy! The reason was the presence of God. When He got on the scene, holiness was a result, even in the ground. **Holiness is a derived experience.** The ground got its holiness from the "being" presence of God. This is exactly what Jesus is trying to tell us. *Being perfect* will come because He has fulfilled the law and come to indwell us. It is derived from Christ *being* what He wants to be within us. Our responsibility is **surrender** to Him.

However, Jesus is not one to overlook the trouble areas. He gives a list in Matthew 5:21-47 which includes six trouble spots that we are going to have to have victory over if we arrive at the destination of verse 48. It is interesting that most of our spiritual problems can be traced back to one of these trouble areas. It is also interesting to note that every one of these trouble areas has to do with our attitudes and our thinking processes. If we do not make the grade in our thought life and our attitudes, there is no chance of making it. Here in the mind is where the Christ-saturation is going to have to be at its best.

Each trouble area is divided into two parts. "You have heard" is the Old Testament tradition that the Jews were familiar with. It was the Law of Moses. "But I say" is the new, fulfilled standard which is going to take precedence. It is going to be a new way through total surrender and indwelling.

TROUBLE AREA NUMBER ONE
(Matthew 5:21-22)

*"You have heard that it was said to those of old,
'You shall not murder, and whoever murders will be
in danger of the judgment.' But I say to you that
whoever is angry with his brother without a cause
shall be in danger of the judgment. And whoever says
to his brother, 'Raca!' shall be in danger of the council.
But whoever says, 'You fool!' shall be in danger of
hell fire."*

"You have heard" (Matthew 5:21) — The old-timer would come along and brag about the fact that he had not been guilty of committing murder. He hated a lot, but he was able to curb the end result of hatred, which would be outward expression. He would sit around and make plans, but he just never carried them out.

"But I say" (Matthew 5:22) — Jesus came and took this old-time law and did two things to it. He intensified it and internalized it. The old-timer said that one should not kill, but Jesus said that one had better not *think kill*. Here Jesus has brought to light the trouble area of our relationships with one another. The problem is in our attitude one to another. Unless we can maintain proper attitudes in our relationships with our fellowmen, we will never arrive at the *being* state of verse 48. The attitude must be constantly surrendered to Christ and kept saturated by His person.

TROUBLE AREA NUMBER TWO
(Matthew 5:27-28)

"You have heard that it was said to those of old,
'You shall not commit adultery.' But I say to you that
whoever looks at a woman to lust for her has already
committed adultery with her in his heart."

"You have heard" (Matthew 5:27) — The old-timer was pleased with himself when he could brag about how he had never been unclean in his sex life. Of course, he sat around, lusted a lot, and wished that he could get involved; but due to the restraints around him, he stayed pure.

"But I say" (Matthew 5:28) — Again, Jesus had internalized and intensified the old-time law. Jesus said that we must not be pure just in the outward sex life; we must be pure in the thinking process of our sex life. If we cannot be pure in our thinking, we cannot be pure.

This trouble area, our relationship with the opposite sex, affects the complete activity of the life. For instance, a teen will ask what is wrong with going to the theater. I know that we have given lots of reasons that have not necessarily registered with the teen. However, I came to a conviction in my own life concerning the theater based upon the basic theme of the theater, and this is sex. I discovered that the show stimulates my thinking process, which turns into lust, which moves me in the direction of outward action. I also learned that while I could handle it once, twice, and three times, eventually it became a pattern of thinking which kept me from arriving at *being* perfect. Through total surrender, I have "Be Perfect" as a goal for my life. I want that so badly that it is desperation in my life. Therefore, anything that disturbs my chance of *being* perfect has to go. If one does not care whether verse 48 is his state or not, then this is not valid for him. But we must all know that the state of *being* perfect must be maintained if heaven is to be experienced.

The same basic truth applies to television. It is not just seeing how much one can get by with; rather the constant indwelling presence of Christ maintaining inward purity is the goal. Consequently, there are some television programs that should be avoided because of the thinking process that is affected. There is liberty that must be granted in some of these areas. Because of the differences in our personalities and past lives, what may be detrimental to the thinking process of one may not be for another. But let's not use this as a cop-out.

A teenager may ask "What's wrong with dancing?" Again, the church has used all kinds of arguments which have broken down due to changing circumstances. We have said that the environment is bad. But dancing has been fostered by the school and some churches, in clean settings. So the argument has been broken down. I have discovered for my life that dancing is wrong. The reason centers in sex. The actions that are done on the dance floor (even in a "clean" setting) are the same actions that are done by the local go-go girl at the swing bar to entertain men. This stimulates the thinking process, which turns into lust, which produces action. Thus verse 48 is violated. I want to *be* perfect. I desperately desire the standard of verse 48. It is not that "I can't" as much as "I won't."

The area of dress seems to be a real issue. What I am concerned about is not the compromising of previously held positions, or the loss of past traditions. I am concerned about the achievement of, and the maintaining of, the *be perfect* state. While the young lady's dress may not affect her thinking process in terms of lust, she has an obligation toward others. If you have the attitude of just doing what you want to, regardless of others, then this will not be valid for you. But if you really desire the state of *being perfect*, you will want to do everything you can to guard the thinking process of yourselves and others. If we do not keep clean in the thinking process, we will not be pure.

TROUBLE AREA NUMBER THREE
(Matthew 5:31-32)

"Furthermore it has been said, 'Whoever divorces his wife, let him give her a certificate of divorce.' But I say to you that whoever divorces his wife for any reason except sexual immorality causes her to commit adultery; and whoever marries a woman who is divorced commits adultery."

"You have heard" (Matthew 5:31) — This trouble area is that of relationship within the marriage. The old-timer would simply be unhappy with his wife and would go down to the representative of Moses' law and get a divorce. It was so easy, for the man had all the rights. Perhaps because of burnt toast or because he felt like it, he would get a divorce.

"But I say" (Matthew 5:32) — But Jesus says the fulfilled law is not that easy. In fact, there can be no divorce without a cause. The only proper cause is fornication, which is unfaith-fulness in the sex life. Now the important thing here is not to prove anything about someone who is already divorced. The important teaching here is for that person who is not married yet, or who is married and isn't divorced. Jesus is saying that when we go into marriage, we must go into it with the awareness that there is no out save for the one cause. One must live with drunkenness, meanness, dirty feet, and a thousand other things. When my wife and I got married we agreed to take the word divorce and strike it from our vocabulary. We would not talk about or even mention it. It is not an answer. This is the new, fulfilled law.

TROUBLE AREA NUMBER FOUR
(Matthew 5:33-34)

*"Again you have heard that it was said to those of old,
'You shall not swear falsely, but shall perform your
oaths to the Lord.' But I say to you,
do not swear at all ..."*

"You have heard" (Matthew 5:33) — The old-timer could not be trusted to do what he said he would do unless one could get him down to the Temple to give his oath over something that was sacred. It was only the promise that the Lord was involved in that he was obligated to keep.

"But I say" (Matthew 5:34) — Jesus said, "Swear not at all." Now some have tried to make this mean that we were not to go into court and swear to tell the truth. But Jesus was not talking about court; rather He was speaking about meaning what you say. This is the trouble area of our word or conversation. When you say it, then you should do it. Your word should be a responsible, honest word. You obligate yourself whether it is an oath over something sacred or not. Your word should mean something. Jesus goes on to say, "Let your communication be, yea, yea; nay, nay." This again is a thinking-process trouble. Because we say something, it ought to be thought over and backed up by our actions.

TROUBLE AREA NUMBER FIVE
(Matthew 5:38-39)

"You have heard that it was said, 'An eye for an eye and a tooth for a tooth.' But I tell you not to resist an evil person. But whoever slaps you on your right cheek, turn the other to him also."

"You have heard" (Matthew 5:38) — The old-time law emphasized justice in terms of the spirit of revenge. However, there was a limit placed upon the revenge that one could collect. If an eye had been taken then one had the right to collect any eye in revenge. If a tooth had been knocked out, then one had the right to knock out one tooth in revenge. No more; just one could be collected.

"But I say" (Matthew 5:39) — Jesus in His fulfilled law came forth with a brand new principle. In this trouble area concerning our relationship with others in the matter of revenge, one is required to not only resist evil, but to turn the other cheek. Some have viewed this as making the Christian out to be a sucker. It means that the Christian always gets the raw end of the deal. He becomes a floor mat for everyone to walk on. If one takes this view concerning these verses, there is real difficulty in reconciling the life of Jesus to these words. Jesus was not a floor mat. He blazed into the Temple and cleaned house with the force of one who was in command! Yes, He may have appeared to be a sucker on the Cross, but before He got done, He created a masterful force of power that whipped sin once and for all.

If one follows through with Jesus' teachings in each one of these trouble areas, one must come back to attitude and the thinking process. The important thing is not being a sucker, but maintaining a proper attitude toward your brother when he has done or is doing wrong to you. Even in the midst of the forceful acts of Jesus, there was a proper attitude maintained. It is interesting that we normally strike back only when we are mad. It is not always wrong to strike back; there are times when we need to take a stand for the right. The problem is in the attitude with which we take that stand. Even in taking our stand, we must demonstrate an attitude of selflessness and concern for others.

TROUBLE AREA NUMBER SIX
(Matthew 5:43-44)

"You have heard that it was said, 'You shall love your neighbor and hate your enemy.' But I say to you, love your enemies, bless those who curse you, do good to those who hate you, and pray for those who spitefully use you and persecute you ..."

"You have heard" (Matthew 5:43) — The old-timer could love those who loved him, and those whose personalities especially clicked with his. But those enemies or persons who did not agree with him, he was free to hate. This is the trouble area of our relationship with our enemies.

"But I say" (Matthew 5:44) — Again, the new fulfilled law through the person of the Indwelling Spirit is the attitude of love at all times. An enemy comes to curse you. The only way he knows to fight is with his fists in a carnal manner. Jesus is saying that there is a new area for the mane in the fulfilled law. It is the area of love, which is a higher plane. It isn't that the person in the fulfilled law gives in and is a coward. No, the person in the fulfilled law fights back, but he fights back on a high plane with the weapons of love. The enemy knows nothing about this kind of warfare and is destroyed, broken, and whipped by this warfare. If we fight back on his ground, we have gained nothing, but when we fight with the new weapon, we conquer him!

The conclusion of the matter is this: "Be pure." This involves not just doing pure things, but a *being* experience of the person of Christ indwelling our lives, sharing His purity with us. There are six trouble areas that we must constantly guard. They all touch the areas of the thinking process and attitudes. Here the person of Jesus within us shines at His best until we are at verse 48, by His grace, *being* "perfect."

Be Pure
Matthew 5:17-48

Be Perfect
(5:48)

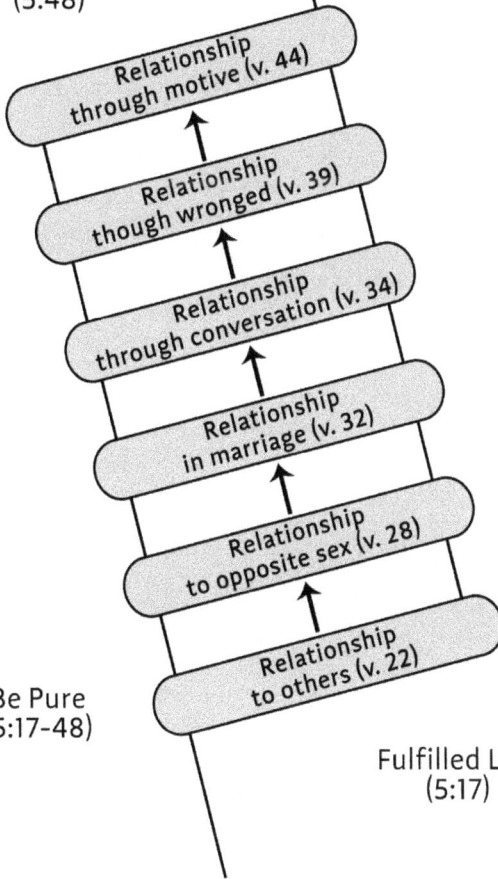

Relationship
through motive (v. 44)

Relationship
though wronged (v. 39)

Relationship
through conversation (v. 34)

Relationship
in marriage (v. 32)

Relationship
to opposite sex (v. 28)

Relationship
to others (v. 22)

Be Pure
(5:17-48)

Fulfilled Law
(5:17)

IV

BE A WITNESS

*But you shall receive power when the Holy Spirit has
come upon you; and you shall be witnesses to Me
in Jerusalem, and in all Judea and Samaria,
and to the end of the earth.*

– Acts 1:8 –

It is amazing that as one begins to comprehend even in a small way this *being* concept of Christianity, one sees it everywhere in every area of life. Acts 1:8 is a scripture that has high status among evangelical Christians as a verse to memorize. It is a verse that has been used as a "whipping post" for those lazy Christians who were lagging behind in their witnessing duty. It is a verse that has stood for the teaching of the fullness of the Holy Spirit. Then I saw it one day! Right in the middle of this verse is the secret to the fullness of Christianity and the winning of a world to Christ! "And you shall be witnesses unto me."

This verse is teaching us a state of *being*, not a state of *doing*. As with purity, one is not to be busy DOING witnessing; rather it is the new flow of BEING a witness. There is a vast difference between the two. "Doing" witnessing is rote memorization of formulas, while "being" a witness is sharing a living love experience.

"Doing" witnessing builds the pride and ego, while "being" a witness builds the image of Christ in the eyes of men. "Doing" witnessing is concerned by the number of times, while "being" a witness is concerned with sharing love.

If "doing" is at the center of our witnessing, there are immediately projected in our pathway several pitfalls. One of these pitfalls is found in the word "how." "How do I do this witnessing?" is the supreme question. From then on it is a series of training classes followed by the memorization of formulas and practice sessions. Understand that there is nothing basically wrong with all of this, yet it all centers in "doing." For many people, it becomes totally discouraging since they try to fit into the pattern established by someone else and just cannot make it.

For instance, in one church it was Brother Jones who was high up on the witnessing scale. When one got saved, he immediately tried to witness like Brother Jones, but that was impossibility. Consequently, the rest of the church found itself sitting back, lacking the sharing experience because they could not do it like Brother Jones. This is one of the falsehoods of "doing" witnessing. You do not have to do it like Brother Jones does it. You *must not* do it like Brother Jones does it. You must do it like *you* do it. The "doing" witness would tend to fit us all into one formula. We would come out as regimented soldiers instead of individual personalities filled with the presence of God, "being" witnesses. My personality can be filled with Christ. When He shines out of my personality, I will be unique from anyone else. It comes from relaxation and surrender to His presence as I am *being* a witness.

A second great pitfall of the "doing" witnessing is the division of our activities. We have come up with two sections — the religious activity and the nonreligious activity. Of course, the nonreligious activities are many. They consist of those daily routine tasks that most of us find ourselves doing in caring for a family. Washing dishes, mowing lawns, working in the factory, going about our daily business are all a part of this list. The religious acts are those spiritual activities such as prayer, Bible reading, witnessing, and preaching. It stands to reason that with these divisions as they are, the more religious a man is, the more religious activities will fill his time.

It is most significant that, even back in the days of the Reformation, Martin Luther knew better that this. He came forth with the concept of the sacredness of every man's vocation. The Bible says that we are to do *everything* that we do to the glory of God! Every action is to be the outgrowth of His presence. Ephesians tells that we are His "workmanship." Our lives, on a 24-hour basis, are to be produced by God; thus totally sacred. This means that milking the cows is as sacred an act as singing in the church or preaching a sermon.

I am convinced that there is a brand-new experience for many of us in terms of witnessing. Witnessing should not be something we have to do; it should be that which we cannot keep from doing! It is not a state of *doing*; rather it is a state of *being*. It is that indwelling presence of Christ in a man's life, sharing Himself through that life all the time. It becomes the expression of the total personality — a continual witness!

There is a tremendous illustration of this in Acts 4:13-14. These verses are the outgrowth of the events in chapter 3. Peter and John, by the power of God, had healed the lame man who sat at the temple. He, of course, had spread their fame everywhere. Peter and John had ended up in prison. These verses that we are dealing with come to light when Peter and John are brought out of prison and the high officials are examining them about the power that they have to do such miracles. These verses are observations made by the unbelievers as they view Peter and John.

JESUS CHRIST
(Acts 4:13)

"Now when they saw the boldness of Peter and John, and perceived that they were uneducated and untrained men, they marveled. And they realized that they had been with Jesus."

There is a progression that is built in verse 13. The verse begins on the exterior of these disciples and then gradually moves to the heart of what is really going on in their lives. It is found at the end of the verse, "that they had been with Jesus." At the very center of this *being* experience is this Person Jesus Christ. He is the One. The unbeliever observed that the disciples had been with Jesus, but in reality, they were with Jesus at that moment. What the scribes and high priest were seeing was the person of Christ being a witness within the lives of these men. The unbeliever became aware of Jesus Christ.

This is the great desire of the gospel for your life. We have many things that we seem to go after in Christianity, but in reality, we need only on thing — one Person, and

His name is Jesus. For the person of Christ to become so central in our lives that others around us become aware of His influence through us is the singular goal of Christianity. This kind of *being* state can never become a reality until He is totally central. The life must revolve around Him. We must be able to say with Paul that "for me to live is Christ."

WEAK INSTRUMENTS — YIELDED
(Acts 4:13)

"Now when they saw the boldness of Peter and John, and perceived that they were uneducated and untrained men, they marveled. And they realized that they had been with Jesus."

We are moving outwardly from the most central thing. Next on the list one finds that the disciples were just weak instruments. In fact, the verse says that they were "unlearned and ignorant men" (KJV). It was so true that the Pharisees had to marvel at what was going on in their lives. These weak instruments did have one secret, and that was their surrender to Christ. What was happening was what Jesus was doing in their lives. This is the key to the *being* state. It is allowing Jesus to be what He wants to be within your life. Through surrender, you become a stage upon which He can act.

The weight of the *being* is upon Him, not upon you. How many times have we used the word "can't"? We have looked at ourselves to note that we are only weak — "unlearned and ignorant"; therefore we can't. Yet these are the very people Christ wants. Those are the kind that He will use the most effectively for the Kingdom. In fact, it is the *only* kind He can use. Weak instruments, yielded, are on the top. Here is involved the dependency of our whole lives upon Him. This must be an attitude of constant living. It produces a relaxed Christian life. It removes one from the trying and striving group into the class of rest. It really does not mean that one has less action; rather there is actually more. Only the action now is not you, but He who had come to be within you.

ATTITUDES
(Acts 4:13)

"Now when they saw the boldness of Peter and John, and perceived that they were uneducated and untrained men, they marveled. And they realized that they had been with Jesus."

The very first of the verse says, "Now when they saw the boldness of Peter and John." This is phrased in an interesting way. These disciples had been speaking and answering the questions of the Pharisees, yet the boldness was something they "saw" instead of "heard." In other words, the emphasis here was not upon what the disciples said as much as on how they said it. It was attitude that impressed these Pharisees. I have found this to be true in every witnessing experience. The first and most lasting influencing factor upon the lives of people is our attitudes.

Would we dare back ourselves into a corner and seriously examine our attitudes? If Christ being within us does not work here, then it just will not work. A Christian teenage girl is trying to win her mother to Christ. She witnesses and prays, but to no avail. What she fails to realize is that her witness is not being heard as much as the attitude she has when her mother asks her to please clean up her room. A Christian wife wants desperately to win her unsaved husband for Christ. She has prayed and witnessed to no avail. The problem is not in the words used, but that which the husband sees first of all — attitude. It is the attitude toward the pastor and the church. It is the attitude during those periods of "nagging." It is not so much what people hear as what they see in your attitude.

OUTWARD DEMONSTRATION
(Acts 4:14)

"And seeing the man who had been healed standing with them, they could say nothing against it."

It is interesting to note that this is the very last. Most of us want to start here; the Bible progression is that we end here. This is the cherry on top of the sundae. After one has become totally surrendered to Christ, the attitude gets right. When the attitude gets right, the outward act of actually witnessing to a person will automatically follow. The disciples had been sharing with their attitudes, and now they could turn to their undisputable evidence of the power of God. For in verse 14, the lame man who had been healed was standing right there. He was their outward demonstration. There was nothing else that could be said. This evidence stopped the mouths of the Pharisees; it settled all the arguments. We need this kind of demonstration. I am convinced that it will naturally follow the one who is *being* a witness.

I want to encourage you to examine your life in view of these facts. Go over these steps again in honesty and let witnessing be a *being* experience for you!

Be a Witness
Acts 4:13-14

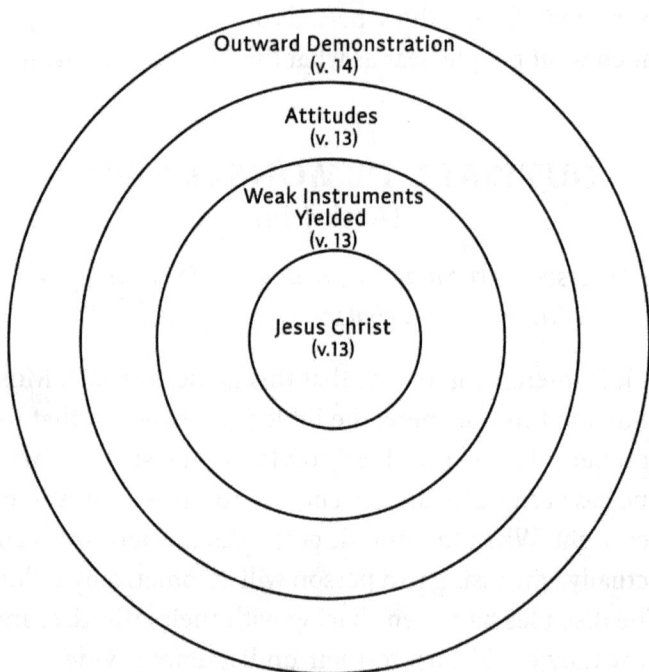

Outward Demonstration
(v. 14)

Attitudes
(v. 13)

Weak Instruments
Yielded
(v. 13)

Jesus Christ
(v.13)

V

BE A LOVER

Love is a contemporary word that has lost its meaning. Its meaning is lost due to its shifting content. Love covers a multitude of emotions, from the lust of immoral acts to the devotion of the saint. The problem is not in the word, but in the content. The content of love needs to be revitalized by the "being" experience. One must locate love in its purest form and possess it. Or perhaps it would be better stated that love in its purest form must possess us. This takes us back to the discovery of love.

Let us go on a search through 1 John 4:8-17. It is here that one discovers the love sandwich. I call it the "love sandwich" because of my past training. My father taught me how to raid the refrigerator at night. If one is going to do it, it ought to be done right. The sandwich to make at such a time is the old Dagwood sandwich, which has everything but the kitchen sink thrown in. It is gigantic in size and stretches the jaws if it is to be devoured. Such a sandwich is this love sandwich. Its content is high, but pure in its form. If your personality will open up in its wildest surrender, you may possess love.

GOD IS LOVE
(1 John 4:8, 16)

He who does not love does not know God, for God is love. . . . And we have known and believed the love that God has for us. God is love, and he who abides in love abides in God, and God in him.

Every sandwich has bread content to it. This is the stabilizer which keeps the rest of the sandwich held together. The bread content to the love sandwich is "God is love." Note that in the scripture, it is spoken of twice, as if it is really significant. For many, it does not mean too much, because they lack understanding. But we *must* understand. The very first touch that one has of God's love is found here — "God is love."

What one discovers in this bread content is a *being* experience on God's part. Love is not something God does; rather it is something He is. It is not that He does certain acts which are lovely; rather, welded into His system is love as content. It is not that God possesses a quality or characteristic called love; rather this love possesses Him. One cannot touch God at any point but what one touches love. He is totally saturated and infiltrated by this *being* love. In fact, it cannot be conceived how He could do any act contrary to love, since the total source of His output *is* love. Do not misunderstand. He is not an easy touch; pure love and compromise do not run together. There is strength for right found in this pure love.

John says that "God is love." God is the only One that it is proper to say this about. "God is love" or "Love is God" is quite proper. No one else can fit into that classification.

One might look at others and see acts of love done. They may express love toward certain persons, so that you might be led to say, "That person is love." But then to say, "Love is that person", means that not only certain parts but his total life is saturated and possessed by love. It means that not one point of "non-love" can be found. Indeed, only God "is love."

But to understand properly, one must comprehend one more fact. God is God, which means He is self-sufficient. You do not add anything to Him, because He cannot acquire anything. He has all of the riches and goodness within Himself. This means that, when God loves me, He loves me for nothing. He loves me for myself. God does not love me because He needs me; rather He needs me because He loves me.

He loves with no strings attached. Nicky Cruz, on the streets of New York City as a gang leader, put a switch blade at the throat of David Wilkerson, the country preacher. Nicky said that he was going to cut the preacher up in little pieces all over the street. David Wilkerson answered that, even if he did, every little piece would love him! That is love for nothing, love with no conditions. So much of our love is conditional love. "I will love you as long as you love me" we state. "Come to church and be good. I will love you then", we offer. But not God! His love is unconditional! If He has loved you for nothing (no gain), then He must love you for yourself alone. Nothing you do or do not do will destroy that love. No failure on your part will ever cause it to end. Is it any wonder Paul screams out in Romans 8: 35, "Who shall separate us from the love of Christ?" This does not mean "once saved, always saved", but it does mean that at the heart of the universe there is an aggressive Lover who is in love with you REGARDLESS! Love without reason and without end is His love, for "God is love."

GOD'S LOVE ACTED
(1 John 4:9-10)

In this the love of God was manifested toward us, that God has sent His only begotten Son into the world, that we might live through Him. In this is love, not that we loved God, but that He loved us and sent His Son to be the propitiation for our sins.

Note that, since this love is such a possessive love, it had to act. God could not sit on His great throne in the sky and just have tickles up and down His spine about us. No, since love possesses Him, it reaches out and kicks Him off His throne into action. This action was an act of self-forgetfulness. He forgot Himself in favor of us. It was a great sacrifice, but love required it. Why did God die for mankind when He knew that many would not accept Him? We have not understood this because we have not understood God's love. He sacrificed because He loved — no strings attached. Your response to Him was not a determining factor, for His love demanded that He act in sacrifice. Regardless of what you do or do not do, one fact remains: God loves you and moved upon that love in great sacrifice to Himself.

RECIPIENTS
(1 John 4:11)

Beloved, if God so loved us, we also ought to love one another.

In verse 11, John calls us the "beloved." In Ephesians 1: 6, the Apostle Paul says, "...wherein He hath made us accepted in the beloved." This is a classification that you fit into. You are an object of God's love action. The Israelites had this concept; they considered themselves the favorites of God and the object of His love. God's love has acted and you have become the recipient of His love.

RESPONSE
(1 John 4:11)

Beloved, if God so loved us, we also ought to love one another.

Sandwiched in this *being* experience of God's love is a strong pull for response. Love is like that. Love desires the possession of its object. But here in the love sandwich, the love possession that God wants in your life will express itself toward others. It is not God and you getting together and living happily ever after. The response that He wants from your heart is love back to Him which will express itself toward others. He goes on to explain how this works in the rest of the sandwich. You will note that this is a sauce in the sandwich which spreads its taste throughout the whole.

LOVE PERFECTED
(1 John 4:12)

No one has seen God at any time. If we love one another, God abides in us, and His love has been perfected in us.

Love is left incomplete until it possesses its object. It is difficult to imagine that God, who needs nothing, has put Himself in the position where He does need someone — and it is you. God does not love you because He needs you; rather He needs you because He loves you. He has taken the risk of His love going unfulfilled and placed Himself where He may be left dangling.

INDWELLING
(1 John 4:13)

By this we know that we abide in Him, and He in us, because He has given us of His Spirit.

Notice that the perfection of God's love as shared in verse 12 is God dwelling within us. This is the height and the completion of His total love program. This is where His love has been heading. This brings us back to the *being* experience of Christ in you. Note that this is the meat of the sandwich. It is amazing to me that everywhere one turns in the Word of God this same *being* experience is found. You were built with the intention of God indwelling your body. It is the perfection of God's love for you.

JESUS CHRIST
(1 John 4:14-15)

*And we have seen and testify that the Father has
sent the Son as Savior of the world.
Whoever confesses that Jesus is the Son of God,
God abides in him, and he in God.*

Now this indwelling centers in the person of God as revealed in Jesus Christ. Jesus is central; He *must* be central in our lives. He is the Heart of the redemption program, the Expression of God's love for us, and the indwelling Person who now possesses our life. Jesus Christ is our Life! Paul expressed it by stating, "For to me to live is Christ."

GOD IS LOVE
(1 John 4:16)

*And we have known and believed the love that God
has for us. God is love, and he who abides in love
abides in God, and God in him.*

All is this, of course, is simply because "God is love." "God is love", which is the kind of love that demanded action on His part. He acted in our behalf, and now is waiting for love responding back from us. As we respond, His love finds its perfection by indwelling us through the Spirit of the person of Christ.

This sandwich must be digested by you. First of all, it ought to be a mental process. You need to understand mentally what has taken place. As you understand with your mind, you ought to experience it with your heart.

Devouring this sandwich would mean the fullness of Christ *being* within your life.

ALIKE
(1 John 4:17)

Love has been perfected among us in this:
that we may have boldness in the day of judgment;
because as He is, so are we in this world.

Every sandwich that is worth eating is the kind that you must put elbows on the table and lean over the plate in order to eat. When you bite into one end, the juices should run out the other! These are called drippings. This love sandwich has some outstanding drippings!

The actual dripping is found in verse 17. It states, "Because as He is, so are we in this world." That is quite a statement! One might rationalize and say that one day, when He appears, we shall be like Him. But John states it in present-tense form. One might rationalize that we could be like He is in some monastery, but John states that "as He is, so are we." Right out there on the street is where this thing works! Right down at your job where you rub shoulders with the world is the test! This is holiness at its height. As God is, so are you to be.

How is He? "God is love." God is unconditional Love. Love with no strings attached has possession of Him. Love which acted in sacrificial ways at its own expense was His love. You are to be just like that. Oh, but I know you just cannot do it like He does it. That is why it is a *being* experience; that is why it must be God dwelling within you, simply *being* love through you. The *being*

62

experience that God has with love now becomes yours as you possess Him. The key is the possession of Him who is Love.

How desperate the world, our neighbors, and our families are for this kind of love! You see, that teenager who acts up in your Sunday school class has never experienced love with no strings attached. All the love he has known ended up to be selfish in the final result. People have been nice to him but only when they wanted to use him. This teen hears "God is love", but he cannot understand it because he has not experienced it. He needs to begin his experience of it by knowing it through you. The very same unconditional love in quality and quantity has come to "be" within you and is now shared to that teen until he will come to bow at the feet of Christ for himself.

Your neighbor needs to taste this kind of love also. He has known the other so-called love. It ended up with selfish motives exposed. He has seen the church member who wanted him to come to church, but only to win a contest. He was not the object of love, but the means to a prize. He has experienced the so-called concern of the Christian who witnessed to him That Christian was more interested in gaining "Brownie" points with God through his witnessing than he was in seeing lives changed. Your neighbor needs to know of the love of God which has no selfish motives attached. Concern which will love regardless of his smoking, swearing, or even rejection is love with no stings attached. How will he ever know that love unless it is shared through you? Not that it would be seen in lovely actions, but in attitude and spirit as Christ has come to "be" love within your life. "As He is, so are we in this world." *Be* a lover.

Be a Lover
1 John 4:8-17

God Is Love (v. 8)	Bread
God's Love Acted (vv. 9-10)	Pickles
Recipients (v. 11)	Tomatoes
Response (v. 11)	Sauce
Love Perfected (v. 22)	Lettuce
Indwelling (v. 13)	Meat
Jesus Christ (vv. 14-15)	Sauce
God Is Love (v. 16)	Bread
Alike (v. 17)	Drippings

STUDY GUIDE

Be a Christian

DAY 1

1. Name the two concepts of thinking found in the Evangelical Church which are in distinct contrast to each other.

2. Which of these two concepts is false?

3. In one paragraph, explain how an unknown circumstance or crucial moment can cause defeat when we live under this false concept.

4. Which of these concepts is true?

5. John 14:6 says:

6. 1 John 5:12 says:

7. What is a by-product of the presence of Jesus?

8. You do not need:
   a.

   b.

   c.

   d.

   e.

   f.

   g.

9. The need of your life is singular. You need:

10. Spend five minutes meditating on the Jesus within you and how He leaves you needing nothing.

DAY 2

1. Memorize Colossians 1:27

2. What is the result of the indwelling of a personal Christ inside your body?

3. Everything before verse 27 tells us:

4. Everything after verse 27 tells us:

5. Colossians 1:13-26 is a description of who Jesus is. Match the following, using your Bible and the Scripture verses only for reference.

1. Creator	a. (v. 20)
2. Preeminent	b. (v. 15)
3. Peacemaker	c. (v. 17)
4. Head	d. (v. 20-21)
5. Visible Image	e. (v. 18)
6. Redeemer	f. (v. 16)
7. Reconciler	g. (v. 14)
8. Fullness	h. (v. 19)
9. Consistor	i. (v. 18)
10. Firstborn	j. (v. 15, 18)

DAY 3

Using the book as your guide, write a one sentence description of who Jesus is for each of the following:

1. Redeemer

2. Visible Image

3. Firstborn

4. Creator

5. Consistor

6. Head

7. Preeminent

8. Fullness

9. Peacemaker

10. Reconciler

DAY 4

Results of His Indwelling
Match the following:

1. Completion

a. daily living

2. Quickening

b. constant & consistent state of aliveness

3. Pathway

c. mind

4. Death-Resurrection

d. relaxed living experience

5. Body

e. Christ in His indwelling presence

6. Strength

f. full presence within

7. Reality

g. purity

8. Wisdom

h. future

9. Freedom

i. life

10. Circumcision

j. a living organism who has the same indwelling Christ

DAY 5

Without using the book, fill in the following chart. (Don't worry about verses or order, just list what you can remember from your study.)

Book of Colossians
Central Message *(Colossians 1:27)*:

WHO HE IS

1.

2.

3.

4.

5.

6.

7.

8.

9.

10.

RESULTS OF HIS INDWELLING

1.

2.

3.

4.

5.

6.

7.

8.

9.

10.

ACTIVITY

Explain to a family member or close friend the "Being Concept."

Be Alive

DAY 1

1. Read John 6:47-58

2. What is the most important word in the Gospel of John?

3. It takes precedence over love because:

4. In John 20: 31, John stressed belief because:

5. How many times does John use the word "life" in these verses?

DAY 2

1. In one paragraph explain why John 6:47 is the summary:

2. "Verily, verily" means:

3. What is the one sentence sermon Jesus gave?

4. Explain in your own words when eternal life begins.

5. Meaning to life includes:
   a.

   b.

   c.

6. All these things hinge upon:

7. Convinced belief carries through to:

8. Fill in the blanks:

One does not _____

unless one _____

9. Nothing will suffice in Christianity but:

DAY 3

1. In John 6:48, Jesus begins to build a structure which leads to life. What is the foundation point of the structure?

2. What is God's name?

3. In Hebrew, God's name is a what?

4. The essence of God's being is:

5. Match the following:
   a. He is the Essence of living …
   b. The intricate pattern of His soul's makeup …
   c. This is the Christ …
   d. The One turned to a crowd and said: …
   e. The texture of His being …

   1) … "I am the Bread of Life"
   2) … who confronts our lives
   3) … is life
   4) … that He might BE living in you.
   5) … is living.

DAY 4

Give a brief description of each of the following:

1. Promises (v. 49)

2. Promise fulfilled (v. 51)

3. Preparation (v. 51)

4. Food (v. 55, 48)

5. Eating (v. 56)

6. Indwelling (v. 56)

DAY 5

1. Based on what you have learned in this chapter, fill in the chart from the foundation up:

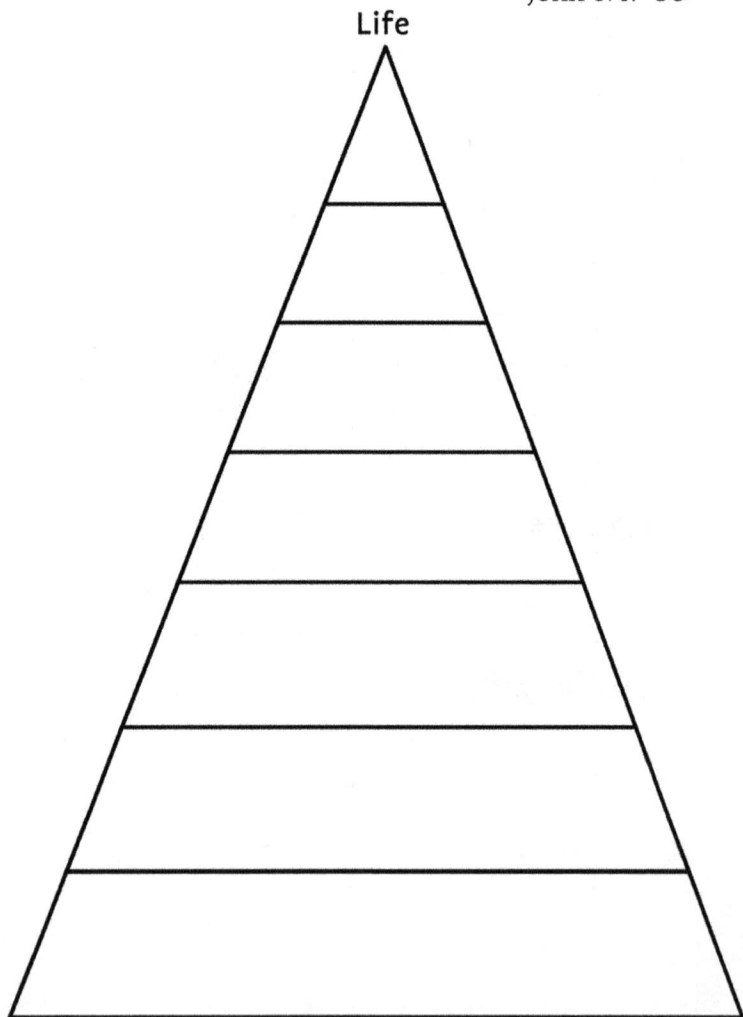

2. Using the author's experience to provoke your thoughts, write in your own words how you will now begin to "practice His presence" and get Christ involved in your daily problems:

3. The indwelling presence of Christ who comes to be life within you will bring:

a.

b.

c.

d.

e.

Be Pure

DAY 1

Mark T for true and F for false.

_____ 1. The Manual is the final word.

_____ 2. A standard called holiness is presented in the Word of God.

_____ 3. In Matthew 5: 48, Jesus says we are to "Be perfect".

_____ 4. "Perfect" means we will never make mistakes.

_____ 5. "Be" means a present state of existence.

_____ 6. Holiness is achieved in terms of quantity of outward actions.

_____ 7. Holiness is a quality of inward life which is a "being state".

_____ 8. The law of God has been done away with.

_____ 9. The law is fulfilled in the person of Christ; He is the standard.

_____ 10. You can live like you want to live.

_____ 11. Jesus relaxed the law of God.

_____ 12. With the indwelling of Christ, the law
is intensified.

_____ 13. Jesus internalized the law and drove it to our
inward parts.

_____ 14. The Old Testament emphasized outward
obedience to the law.

_____ 15. Jesus emphasized inward motive of the heart.

_____ 16. No one can be like Jesus.

_____ 17. Jesus is the keeper of the standard within us.

_____ 18. If we totally surrender to Jesus, He will keep
His law through us.

_____ 19. Jesus instructs us to do perfect things.

_____ 20. Holiness is a derived experience.

DAY 2

Match the following:

"You have heard"

1. You shall not commit adultery

2. You shall love your neighbor and hate your enemies

3. You shall not make false vows, but shall fulfill your vows to the Lord

4. You shall not commit murder

5. Give your wife a divorce if you are unhappy with her

6. An eye for an eye and a tooth for a tooth

"But I say"

a. Don't hate your brother

b. Be pure in your thinking

c. Keep a proper attitude towards your brother even when he wrongs you

d. Think about your words before you speak them; then keep them

e. There is only one cause for divorce: fornication

f. Fight your enemies with with the weapon of love

DAY 3

Fill in the blanks.

1. There is a standard called _____

as presented in the _____ that

settles every question

2. In Matthew 5:48, Jesus states that we must

"Be _____"

3. Jesus says that our perfection is to be like the

_____   _____

_____

4. The standard is _____

5. Perfection is a "_____" state

6. The law is fulfilled in the person of _____

7. We must live like _____ lives

8. Jesus became our _____

9. When Jesus consumed the law into Himself, He

did two things: He _____ and

_____ the law

10. The law is now more _____

than in the OT

11. Jesus has taken the law to our _____

_____

12. In the OT, the emphasis of the law was

_____   _____

13. Now the emphasis is _____

_____

14. The fulfilled law concerns itself with

_____ _____,

which is the _____ of the external

actions

15. The result of the law fulfilled is the

_____ Christ through His Spirit

16. Jesus is the _____ of the law

and the _____ of that standard

within us

17. All we need to do is _____

_____ ourselves to Him and

_____ Him to keep His law

_____ us

DAY 4

1. There is a vast difference between to do perfect things and to "be" perfect. List the differences:

To Do

1)

2)

3)

4)

To "Be"

1)

2)

3)

4)

2. Explain in your own words what the following statement means: "Holiness is a derived experience."

3. Explain how we can "Be" perfect and what our responsibility is.

DAY 5

Name the six trouble areas:

1)

2)

3)

4)

5)

6)

Each of these trouble areas has to do with our attitudes and our thinking processes. Take each area and explain how the Indwelling Christ fulfills the law in us.

1)

2)

3)

4)

5)

6)

STUDY GUIDE
Be a Witness

DAY 1

1. Life is a by-product of the presence of Jesus being what?

2. The need in your life is singular. You need:

3. Convinced belief carries through to:

4. One does not _____ unless one

   _____

5. Nothing will suffice in Christianity but:

6. Holiness is a quality of inward life which is a:

7. _____ is the law fulfilled.

8. When Jesus consumed the law into Himself, what two things did He do to it?

9. Jesus is the one _____ of the

law and the _____ of that

standard within us.

10. With our lives saturated by Christ, we can

"_____ _____,"

as He instructs us in Matthew 5: 48.

DAY 2

1. Acts 1:8 teaches us a state of _____,

not a state of _____.

2. We are not to be busy _____

witnessing, rather we are to have a new flow of

_____ a witness.

3. List the differences between "Doing" and "Being"
Doing
   1)

   2)

   3)

Being
   1)

   2)

   3)

DAY 3

1. One pitfall in "doing" witnessing is "How do I do this witnessing?" Explain in your own words why this is a pitfall.

2. The "doing" witness tends to fit us all into one formula. Explain in your own words how we are to "Be witnesses."

3. Another pitfall in "doing" witnessing is the division of our activities. Explain in your own words what this means.

4. Explain the concept of the sacredness of every man's vocation.

5. Based upon what you have just learned, explain what witnessing means.

DAY 4

Read Acts 4:13-14

Using one paragraph for each numbered item; explain the observation made by the unbelievers as they view Peter and John and how this relates to our lives.

1. Jesus Christ (v. 13)

2. Weak Instruments — Yielded (v. 13)

3. Attitudes (v. 13)

4. Outward Demonstration (v. 14)

DAY 5

Fill in the chart

Be a Witness
Acts 4:13-14

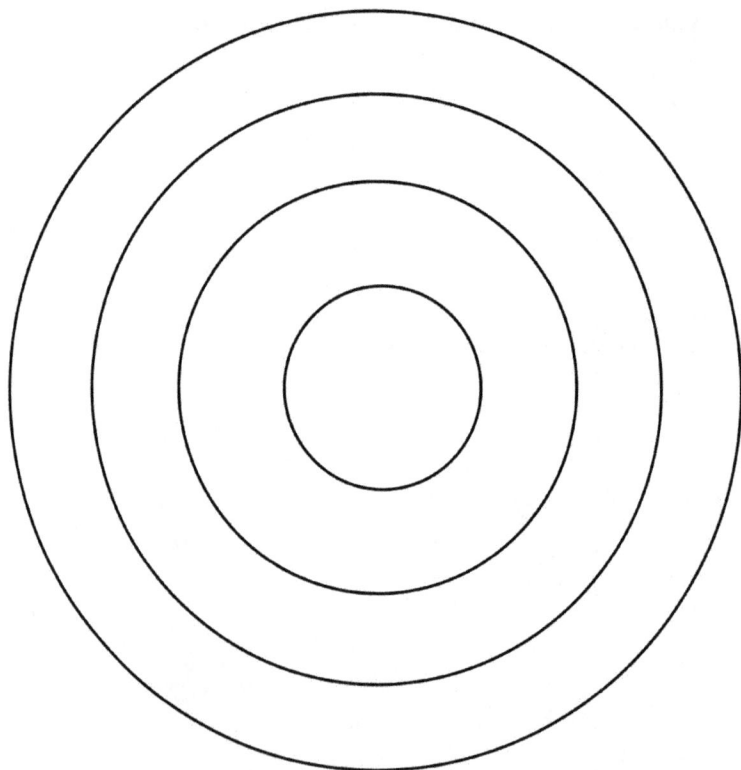

Activity

In honesty, examine your life in view of the facts you have just learned. Meditate on how you are going to let witnessing be a "being experience" for you.

Be a Lover

DAY 1

Circle the number of the true statements.

1. Love is a contemporary word that has lost its meaning.

2. The problem is not in the word, but in the content.

3. All men have experienced love.

4. Love in its purest form must possess us.

5. You can live your own life and experience love.

6. Love is not something God does; rather it is something He is.

7. Pure love and compromise run together.

8. God is an easy touch.

9. Only God "is love".

10. God does not love me because He needs me; rather He needs me because He loves me.

11. You can do certain things to destroy God's love for you.

12. Romans 8: 35 means "once saved, always saved".

13. "Who can separate us from the love of Christ?" means Christ is an aggressive lover who is in love with you regardless.

14. God's possessive love acted when He left His throne to die for me.

15. I am the object of God's love action.

16. My response to God's love means God and I get together and live happily ever after.

17. The response that God wants from my heart is love back to Him which expresses itself toward others.

18. The perfection of God's love is God dwelling within us.

19. Jesus must be central in our lives.

20. Love does not work on the streets.

21. The being experience that God has with love now becomes yours as you possess Him.

DAY 2
Fill in the blanks

1. One must _____ love in its

_____ form and _____ it

2. Love is not something God _____;

rather it is something He _____

3. God's love is _____

4. Since this love is such a possessive love, it had to

_____

5. God's love for us required a great _____

6. You are an _____ of God's love
action

7. God's love has a strong pull for _____

8. The response that God wants from your heart is

love back to Him which _____

_____   _____

_____

9. Love is left _____ until it
possesses its object

10. The perfection of God's love is God _____

_____   _____

11. Jesus is the _____ of the

redemption program, the _____ of

God's love, and the _____

_____ who now possesses our life.

12. As God _____, so are you to

_____

DAY 3

Match the following:

1. The bread content of the love sandwich is

2. Love is not something God does

3. It is not that He does certain acts which are lovely

4. It is not that God possesses a quality or characteristic called love

5. When one touches God at any point

6. "Love is that person" means

7. God does not love me because He needs me

8. If He has loved you for nothing (no gain)

9. Romans 8:35 does not mean "once saved, always saved"

10. Love without reason and without end is His love

a. for God is Love"

b. rather, welded into His system is love as content.

c. then He must love you for yourself alone

d. one touches love

e. rather it is something He is

f. rather He needs me because He loves me

g. His total life is saturated and possessed by love

h. "God is love"

i. rather this love possesses Him

j. but it means God is an aggressive lover who is in love with you REGARDLESS!

DAY 4

Write out a description/summary of each section:

1. God's Love Acted (1 John 4:9, 10)

2. Recipients (1 John 4:11)

3. Response (1 John 4:11)

4. Love Perfected (1 John 4:12)

5. Indwelling (1 John 4:13)

6. Jesus Christ (1 John 4:14, 16)

DAY 5

1. 1 John 4:17 says:

2. When are we to be like Him?

3. Where are we to be like Him?

4. How are we to be like Him?

5. Why are we to be like Him?